Religions of the World

Buddhism

Rita Faelli

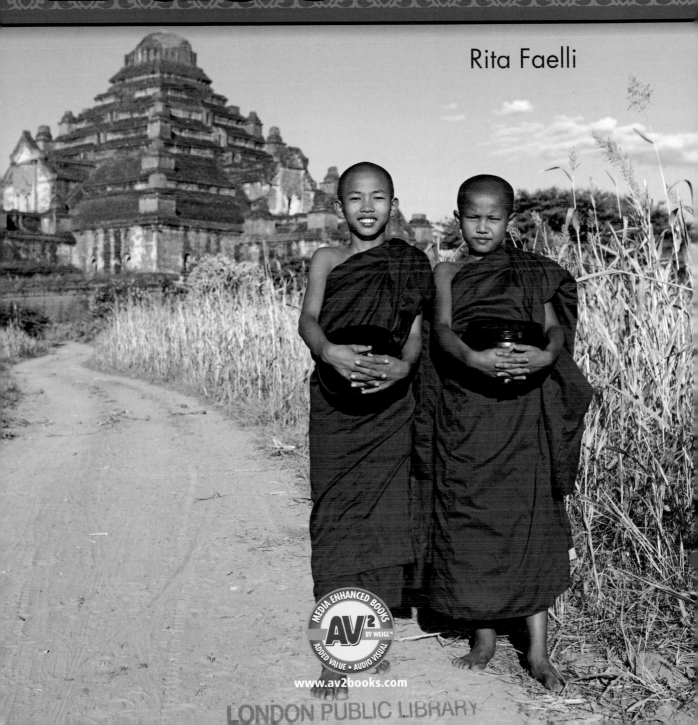

www.av2books.com

AV² provides enriched content that supplements and complements this book. Weigl's AV² books strive to create inspired learning and engage young minds in a total learning experience.

Your AV² Media Enhanced books come alive with...

Audio
Listen to sections of the book read aloud.

Key Words
Study vocabulary, and complete a matching word activity.

Video
Watch informative video clips.

Quizzes
Test your knowledge.

Embedded Weblinks
Gain additional information for research.

Slide Show
View images and captions, and prepare a presentation.

Try This!
Complete activities and hands-on experiments.

... and much, much more!

Go to www.av2books.com, and enter this book's unique code.

BOOK CODE

M 5 8 2 6 2 3

AV² by Weigl brings you media enhanced books that support active learning.

Published by AV² by Weigl
350 5ᵗʰ Avenue, 59ᵗʰ Floor
New York, NY 10118
Website: www.av2books.com

Library of Congress Control Number: 2015942084

ISBN 978-1-4896-4023-9 (hardcover)
ISBN 978-1-4896-4024-6 (soft cover)
ISBN 978-1-4896-4025-3 (single user eBook)
ISBN 978-1-4896-4026-0 (multi-user eBook)

Printed in the United States of America in Brainerd, Minnesota
1 2 3 4 5 6 7 8 9 0 19 18 17 16 15

052015
052215

Photo Credits

The publisher gratefully acknowledges the photo suppliers for this title: iStock, pages 1, 5; Peter Cadman, pages 12, 16b, 20; Buddha Dharma Education Association, pages 14, 15, 29; Irina Evstratova, page 16d; Luke Sharrock, page 23; Marc Lantrok, page 26; Phillip Dyer, page 27. All other photographs and illustrations are © copyright UC Publishing Pty Ltd.

Every reasonable effort has been made to trace ownership and to obtain permission to reprint copyright material. The publishers would be pleased to have any errors or omissions brought to their attention so that they may be corrected in subsequent printings.

Contents

What Is Buddhism?

Buddhism is both a religion and a way of living. It began in India about 2,500 years ago. People who practise Buddhism are called Buddhists.

Buddhists follow the teachings of the **Buddha**. Buddha was an Indian prince called Siddhartha Gautama. He lived in northern India about 2,500 years ago.

Word fact

The word *Buddha* is a special title that means the awakened one – that is, someone who is very wise.

The Tian Tan Buddha in Hong Kong, China, is one of the world's largest Buddha statues. People first started making statues and paintings of Buddha around 100 AD.

Over the centuries, Buddhism spread throughout Asia. Today, Buddhism is also practised by people living in America, Canada, Europe and Australia.

There are many different schools of Buddhism. These schools have different writings and languages and have developed in different cultures. However, all Buddhists share some basic beliefs.

The Three Gems

There are three things that are central to all forms of Buddhism. These are sometimes called the **Three Gems**. The Three Gems are Buddha, the teacher; **Dharma**, the Buddha's teachings or laws; and **Sangha**, the community of monks and nuns.

Buddhists pay respect to the Buddha, learn the Dharma and follow the advice of the Sangha. By doing this, Buddhists believe they can become wise and happy.

7

The story of the Buddha

Siddhartha Gautama was born on the full-moon day of May, around 560 BC. He was a crown prince of a small territory near the Indian-Nepalese border.

Siddhartha had everything he wanted. But he realized there was more to life than just money and possessions.

According to legend, he was riding in his chariot when he saw an old man, a sick man and a corpse by the roadside. This was his first experience with old age, sickness and death. Siddhartha was very shocked. It made him lose all happiness in living.

Siddhartha wanted to find out why there was so much suffering in the world. He decided to leave his palace and all his riches and go in search of life's meaning.

For about ten years, Siddhartha tried many different ways to find the truth. Finally, he decided to stop eating because he believed this would help him find knowledge. He became so weak that he fainted on the roadway. He was discovered by a young girl, called Sujata, who fed him milk and rice cakes. She saved his life.

Siddhartha began meditating under a fig tree. The Buddhists call this the **Bodhi tree** – the tree of wisdom. Sujata continued to bring him food, and a herd boy brought him grass to sit on.

Siddhartha at last found the knowledge he was searching for. Once Siddhartha Gautama understood the truth about life, he became the Buddha. He devoted the rest of his life to sharing his teachings with others.

At first, he only had five followers, but soon he founded an order of monks. For 45 years, he gave public teachings and private advice to his followers. He died in about 480 BC at the age of 80.

After his death, temples were built in his honour, and his religion spread throughout a great part of Asia. Today more than 350 million people all over the world are Buddhists.

The Buddha's Teachings

The Buddha's teachings are called Dharma. Dharma teaches Buddhists how to live with kindness and wisdom.

By following Buddha's teachings, people can reach **enlightenment**.

The Buddha taught that nothing is perfect in this world and that nothing lasts. Buddhists believe that Buddha showed them the right path that leads to the end of suffering.

The Dharma is often symbolized in pictures as a wheel.

Word fact

For Buddhists, enlightenment means having a deep understanding about the way things are. It means being free from jealousy, envy, anger, greed, and selfishness.

For many years, Buddha's teachings were passed on by word. His followers would recite, word for word, what Buddha had said in his teaching. These teachings are called **sutras**.

Hundreds of years later, these sutras were written down. They always begin with the words, "Thus have I heard".

Buddhist holy books have been translated into many languages. The collection of Buddhist writings is called the **Tripitaka**. It includes the sutras, rules and practices for behavior, and writings that discuss and explain the sutras.

Karma

Buddha taught that when you do something bad on purpose, you get a bad action in return. The same is true for good actions. This is called **karma**, the law of cause and effect.

Good actions, such as generosity, honesty, and meditation, will bring happiness. Bad actions, such as lying, stealing or killing, will bring unhappiness. Buddhists believe that we create new karma every moment by what we say, do, and think.

Fast fact

Even a small act of helpfulness, like helping someone with directions, is good karma. There is a Buddhist saying, "Do not overlook tiny good actions, thinking they are of no benefit. Even tiny drops of water will eventually fill a huge vessel."

Meditation

Buddha taught that **meditation** can make you become a better person. Meditation calms the mind and frees it from all thoughts and worries.

Fast fact

A very simple way to meditate is to sit in a comfortable position and concentrate on breathing. Notice your breath going in and out. When you concentrate for a while, your body becomes relaxed and your mind becomes peaceful.

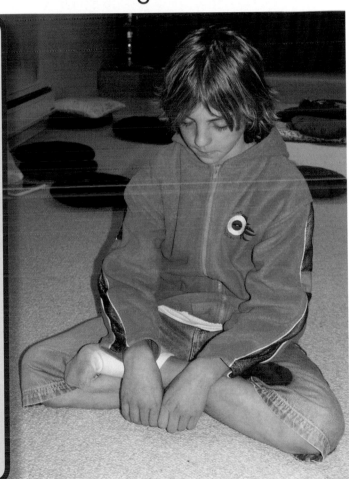

Monks and Nuns

The community of Buddhist monks and nuns is called the Sangha.

Buddhist monks and nuns give all their time to following the teachings of Buddha. They own only a few things, such as robes and an offering bowl. Some monks and nuns shave their heads to show that they do not care about external beauty.

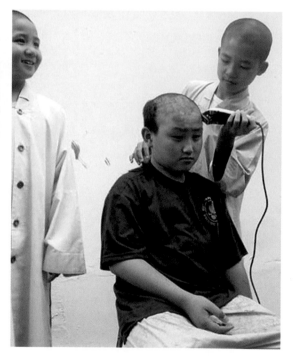

Boys and men training to be monks are called novices. They live in monasteries, places where monks and novices study Buddhism.

Buddhist monks don't take lifetime **vows**. This means that they don't have to be monks for all their lives. Some people only become monks for a short period of time.

Fast facts
Boys as young as eight years old can become novice monks.

The robes of monks and nuns are simple and made from cotton or linen. Their color varies according to the country they are in.

Yellow robes are mostly worn in Thailand, while black robes are worn in Japan. In China and Korea, grey and brown robes are worn for work, while more decorative robes are used for ceremonies. Dark red robes are worn in Tibet.

Offering Food to Monks and Nuns

When people have problems, they go to monks and nuns for advice. As a sign of respect, and to thank them for this advice, people offer monks and nuns food and clothing.

Monks and nuns do not beg for food, but accept whatever is offered. This practice helps the monks and nuns to be humble. It also gives people an opportunity to be generous.

17

Where Do Buddhists Worship?

Buddhist religious buildings are called temples.

Temples always have a **shrine** in them. The Buddha image sits in the centre of the shrine. Candles, incense, and flowers are placed around the Buddha image.

People meditate and perform religious ceremonies in front of a shrine. Before they go into a shrine room, Buddhists take off their shoes to show respect.

Fast facts

Some Buddhists have a shrine in their homes. The home shrine is a place where family members go to meditate, chant, or perform religious ceremonies. Special offerings are made to Buddha to show gratitude and respect.

How Do Buddhists Worship?

There are many ways for Buddhists to worship – praying, chanting, meditating, and making offerings.

Buddhists can chant parts of the holy books, meditate, burn incense and make offerings. Buddhists may greet the image of Buddha by putting the palms of their hands together and touching their chest, lips, and forehead. There is no special day of worship for Buddhists. They can visit a shrine at any time.

Offerings to Buddha

Buddhists make offerings to show their respect to Buddha. The traditional offerings are:

- flowers – these are offered to remind people of how quickly things change

- light from lamps or candles – this symbolizes wisdom

- incense – this reminds people to be peaceful

- water – this represents purity

- food – this reminds people to give their best to Buddha.

Buddha Images

There are many different images of the Buddha. The different Buddha images show different personal qualities.

There are images of the Buddha standing, sitting and even lying down. The Buddha's hands may also be in different positions.

A statue of the Buddha with his hand resting gently in his lap is a reminder to become calm and peaceful. A statue with the Buddha's right hand touching the ground shows determination.

Buddhist Symbols

Buddhist symbols have special meanings that remind followers of the Buddha's teachings. The Buddhist flag, the **mandala**, and the lotus flower are three special symbols.

Buddhists believe that while the Buddha sat under the Bodhi Tree after his enlightenment, six rays of light came out from his body. The colors of the rays were yellow, blue, white, red, orange, and a mixture of all the colors. The Buddhist flag was designed using these colors.

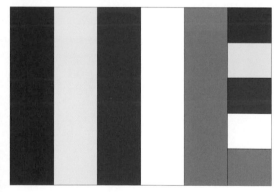

A mandala is a special pattern made up of circles, squares, and triangles.

A mandala is a powerful symbol. It represents wholeness. It is used in ceremonies and to help you pray or meditate.

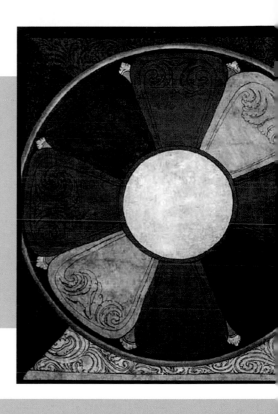

The lotus flower is a common symbol in Buddhism. It represents the enlightened person. There is a poem that describes this enlightenment.

The lotus has its roots in the mud,
Grows up through the deep water,
And rises to the surface.
It blooms into perfect beauty and
purity in the sunlight.
It is like the mind unfolding to
perfect joy and wisdom.

25

Birth

Most Buddhists follow the customs of their country when it comes to family events. But the arrival of a newborn baby is a special occasion for many Buddhists.

In some Buddhist countries, the main ceremony for a newborn baby includes shaving all or some of the baby's head. The hair is a symbol of "bad karma" from a previous life. A monk cuts the hair and blesses the baby.

Marriage

In Buddhist countries, a wedding usually takes place in the bride's home. Sometimes, the celebrations last for several days.

A close relative of the bride usually performs the ceremony. The bride and groom exchange rings. The thumbs of their right hands are tied together. This is a symbol that they are joined as husband and wife.

Sometimes the couple go to the **monastery** before or after the wedding. They listen to the Buddha's teaching on marriage. At the end of the ceremony everyone gets together and celebrates.

Death and Rebirth

Buddhists believe that after people die they are born again, sometimes many times over. The cycle of birth, life, death and rebirth is called **samsara**.

How people are reborn depends on karma. Buddhists believed that the thoughts and actions of this life will shape the next life.

Fast fact

The continuous cycle of birth, life and death is symbolized by the wheel of life.

Buddhist Festivals

Buddha told his followers they should meet together regularly and in large numbers. So festivals are important events in the life of the Buddhist community.

The most important Buddhist festival is in May and is called **Wesak**, or Buddha Day. The celebration honours the birth, enlightenment, and death of the Buddha.

There is a ceremony where scented water is poured over a statue of the baby Siddhartha. This is a symbol of purifying thoughts and actions.

Key Words

Bodhi tree the tree under which Buddha sat when he gained enlightenment. It is also known as the Tree of Wisdom

Buddha a title meaning "Enlightened One", given to Siddhartha Gautama, the founder of Buddhism

Buddhism a religion that is based on the teachings of Buddha

Dharma Buddha's teachings or laws

enlightenment understanding about the meaning and nature of life

karma intended actions and their consequences. Buddhists believe that people's intended actions effect what happens to them in the future

mandala an important Buddhist design and a symbol of wholeness

meditation the practice of emptying the mind of all thoughts and emotions

monastery a place where religious men, called monks, live, work and pray

samsara the cycle of birth, life, death and rebirth

Sangha the Buddhist community of monks and nuns

shrine a small area which has a special religious image or symbol and is used for worship

Sutras teachings given by the Buddha, in his own words

Three Gems the centre of Buddhist beliefs. It consists of the Buddha, his teachings, and the community of monks and nuns

Tripitaka the collection of Buddhist scriptures, or holy writings

vow an important promise

Wesak an important Buddhist festival celebrating Buddha's life, also known as Buddha Day

30

Index

Log on to www.av2books.com

AV² by Weigl brings you media enhanced books that support active learning. Go to www.av2books.com, and enter the special code found on page 2 of this book. You will gain access to enriched and enhanced content that supplements and complements this book. Content includes video, audio, weblinks, quizzes, a slide show, and activities.

AV² Online Navigation

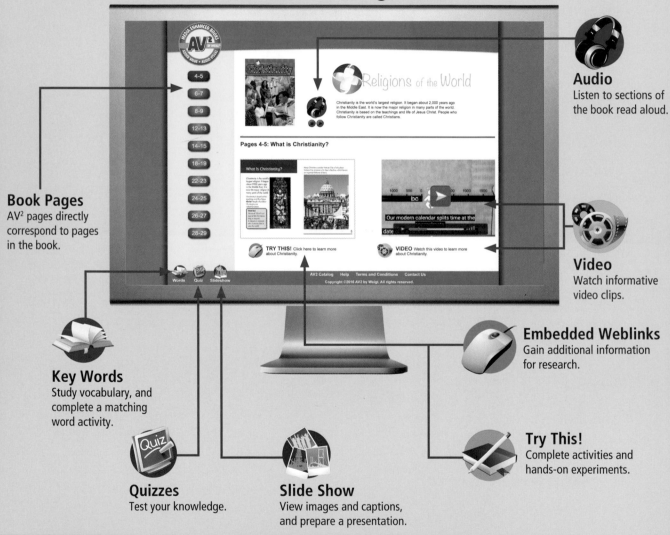

Book Pages
AV² pages directly correspond to pages in the book.

Key Words
Study vocabulary, and complete a matching word activity.

Quizzes
Test your knowledge.

Slide Show
View images and captions, and prepare a presentation.

Audio
Listen to sections of the book read aloud.

Video
Watch informative video clips.

Embedded Weblinks
Gain additional information for research.

Try This!
Complete activities and hands-on experiments.

AV² was built to bridge the gap between print and digital. We encourage you to tell us what you like and what you want to see in the future.

Sign up to be an AV² Ambassador at www.av2books.com/ambassador.